DATE DUE

SEP 1 2 2008	JUN 3 0 2011
MAY 1 3 2009	NOV 1 5 2011
MAY 2 0 2009	FEB 1 1 2012
JUL 0 8 2009	
JUL 2 3 2009	
SEP 1 7 2009	
OCT 0 8 2009	
OCT 2 9 2009	
FEB 1 0 2010	
FEB 1 7 2010	
MAR 3 0 2010	
MAY 2 6 2010	
JUN 1 5 2010	

ico, Inc. 38-293

BIG CATS

JAGUARS

Don Middleton

The Rosen Publishing Group's
PowerKids Press™
New York

This book is dedicated to my wife Sue and my daughters Jody and Kim. Without their support, my writing and other wildlife adventures would not have been possible. Also, a special thanks to author and friend Diana Star Helmer for believing in me.

Published in 1999 by The Rosen Publishing Group, Inc.
29 East 21st Street, New York, NY 10010

First Edition

Book Design: Danielle Primiceri

Photo Credits: Cover © 1996 PhotoDisc, Inc.; p. 5 © Joe Van Os, 1997/The Image Bank; p. 6 © St. Louis Zoo/M.Austerman/Animals Animals; pp. 8, 11, 13, 17, 22 © Shumway, Gail/FPG International; p. 14 © Richard Kolar/Animals Animals; p. 18 © Nicolas Russell/The Image Bank; p. 20 © Kuhn, Lee/FPG Inernational

Middleton, Don.
    Jaguars / by Don Middleton.
        p.   cm. — (Big cats)
    Includes index.
    Summary: Describes the physical characteristics, habits, natural environment, and interrelationship with people of the jaguar and discusses what is being done to preserve it from extinction.
    ISBN 0-8239-5210-X
    1. Jaguar—Juvenile literature. [1. Jaguar.] I. Title. II. Series: Middleton, Don. Big cats.
QL737.C23M5428 1998
599.75'5—dc21
                                                                                                97-43896
                                                                                                CIP
                                                                                                AC

Manufactured in the United States of America

CONTENTS

WILD CATS

Jaguars are one of the four **species** (SPEE-sheez) of "great cats." The others are lions, tigers, and leopards. Only great cats give a mighty roar. Jaguars are larger than leopards but smaller than both lions and tigers.

The jaguar is a close relative of the leopard. But leopards are found only in Africa and Asia. Some **scientists** (SY-en-tists) believe that long ago leopard-like cats traveled from Asia to the Americas. That's how the spotted cats got here. Today, jaguars live in South and Central America. Jaguars were once common in Mexico and the southern United States, but few still live there today.

Even though jaguars can roar, ▶ they hardly ever do.

4

FAMILY OF EIGHT

Jaguars are the largest wild cats found in the Americas. There are eight **subspecies** (SUB-spee-sheez) of jaguars. The Amazon, Panamanian, Parana, Peruvian, and Yucatan subspecies are doing well. Three others have almost disappeared, including the Arizona jaguar. That subspecies once lived in Arizona, Texas, and New Mexico in the United States.

Jaguars are about 30 inches tall and can weigh up to 350 pounds. Their bodies can grow to be five feet long. And their tails are over two feet long. Female jaguars are usually a little smaller than males.

Jaguars look a lot like their cousin, the leopard. But jaguars have a larger head, shorter legs, and bigger spots.

GHOST OF THE FOREST

Jaguars are beautiful wild cats. Their bodies are strong, and they have shorter legs than other big cats. This helps them run and jump through the thick **rain forest** (RAYN FOR-est). Most jaguars have yellow fur covered with black rings and spots. Like their close cousins, the leopards, some jaguars are born with black fur. Jaguars with black fur have spots too. But it's hard to see black spots on black fur. Both black- and yellow-furred cubs can be born in the same **litter** (LIT-ter).

The spotted markings on a jaguar's fur help it to blend in with the many trees and plants that grow in the rain forests where jaguars live.

◀ Just like human fingerprints, the markings on each jaguar's face are different from the markings on all other jaguars' faces.

FANGS AND CLAWS

Jaguars are **fierce** (FEERS) **predators** (PRED-uh-terz). They kill large animals such as deer and **capybaras** (KAP-ee-bar-uhz), which are the largest rodents in the world. Jaguars also eat many smaller animals, including mice and turtles.

A jaguar hunts by surprising its **prey** (PRAY). The jaguar waits in the tall grass or hides on a tree branch and watches for an animal. Then the jaguar springs from its hiding place. It uses its sharp claws to catch and hold its prey. The jaguar bites the animal's throat or head using its fangs, or long front teeth. Jaguars are the only big cats that bite the head of their prey.

For its size, the jaguar has a more powerful bite than any of the other big cats, including tigers. ▶

SECRET LIVES

Jaguars live in rain forests and thick swamps filled with many trees and plants. More than any other big cat, jaguars like to have a river or lake nearby. They are good swimmers and often catch fish to eat. Jaguars also live on open grasslands, in desert-like areas, and even on mountains. Except for mothers with cubs, jaguars always live alone.

Jaguars hunt at night when it is hard for other animals to see them. During the day, they rest on grassy beds or on high tree branches.

12

High up in a tree is one of a jaguar's favorite places to hang out!

BABY JAGUARS

Jaguars usually **mate** (MAYT) between March and September. This way, the jaguar cubs will be born between June and December, when it is not too wet in the rain forest. When mating, a female jaguar leaves a special smell on the ground to attract a male jaguar. After mating, the male leaves. After three to four months, the female may give birth to a litter of one to four cubs.

At birth, jaguar cubs are blind and unable to walk. The little cubs drink their mother's milk to grow big and strong. The mother jaguar hides them deep in the forest. This keeps them safe from hungry predators.

◀ When jaguar cubs are born, they weigh about three pounds each. That's about half the size of a human baby.

GROWING UP

Young jaguars grow up quickly. But for the first three months they are in great danger from other predators. They stay very quiet while their mother goes hunting. When they are about three months old, the cubs start hunting with their mother. She teaches her cubs what animals are good to eat.

Mother jaguars are good teachers. Soon the cubs learn to hunt small animals by themselves. After two years, jaguar cubs leave their mothers and live alone in the rain forest. Jaguars live to be about fifteen to twenty years old in the wild. They can live to be 25 years old in zoos and wildlife parks.

Jaguar cubs learn almost everything they need to know from their mothers. ▶

JAGUARS AND PEOPLE

Jaguars hardly ever attack people. But many people who live near the rain forest are afraid of jaguars. Often, people kill jaguars and other wild cats that come near their town. Wildlife scientists are trying to teach people that they do not have to be afraid of jaguars.

In most countries where jaguars live, there are laws to protect the cats. Hunting is not allowed. But thousands of jaguars are killed **illegally** (il-LEE-gul-lee) by **poachers** (POH-cherz). The poachers sell the fur, claws, teeth, and other parts for lots of money.

◀ People used to wear coats made from jaguar fur. Today that is against the law in most countries.

Jaguars are hard to see because of their coats. Also, jaguars like to travel at night when people are not around.

JAGUARS IN PUBLIC

It is very hard to find jaguars in the wild. For most people, their only chance to see a jaguar is at a zoo. The country of Belize in Central America has a zoo with a large area that looks like a rain forest. Visitors to this zoo can sometimes see the jaguars as they move around.

We need to learn more about how jaguars live in the wild so we can understand them better, and learn how to protect them. Some scientists go into the rain forests to study jaguars. But often, the scientists are not able to find the jaguars. This is because the jaguars' spotted fur blends in very well with the forest.

A FUTURE FOR JAGUARS

While jaguars still live in the rain forests of the Americas, their numbers are going down quickly. In many places, people are cutting down the trees or burning the rain forests to make farms. The jaguars that lived there are forced to find new places to live.

The country of Belize has a large park called the Cockscomb Basin Jaguar Preserve. Jaguars are protected in this large rain forest. Many other countries should do the same thing. All animals, including jaguars need wild places where they can live free and safe.

GLOSSARY

capybara (KAP-ee-bar-uh) The largest rodent in the world. It lives in South America.

fierce (FEERS) Strong and ready to fight.

illegal (il-LEE-gul) Against the law.

litter (LIT-ter) A group of baby animals born to the same mother at the same time.

mate (MAYT) A special joining of a male and female body. After mating, the female may have a baby grow inside her body.

poacher (POH-cher) A person who kills an animal that is protected by law.

predator (PRED-uh-ter) An animal that kills other animals for food.

prey (PRAY) An animal that is killed by another animal for food.

rain forest (RAYN FOR-est) A very wet area that has many kinds of plants, trees, and animals.

scientist (SY-en-tist) A person who studies the way things are and act in the universe.

species (SPEE-sheez) A group of animals that are very much alike.

subspecies (SUB-spee-sheez) A group of animals that are in the same species but have small differences.

WEB SITES:

You can learn more about jaguars at these Web sites:

http://www.primenet.com/~brendel/

http://www.defenders.org/jagua.html

INDEX